The Handbook

For Understanding Your Dreams And Interpreting Them

God Wants To Share His Secrets
With You Through Dreams and Visions

Rev. Dr. Sandra Y. Washington

Integrity Publishing
39343 Harbor Hills Blvd Lady Lake,
FL 32159

www.integrity-publishing.com

CONTENTS

Acknowledgments v

Compliments vii

The Introduction ix

Chapter 1 1

   1. What is Revelation Knowledge and Head Knowledge? 1

   2. The Revelatory Gifts or Manifestations of the Holy
      Spirit that Knows Something 2

   3. The Utterance Spiritual Gifts or Gifts that Say Something 4

   4. The Power Gifts or Manifestation of the Power of the
      Holy Spirit that does Something 5

Chapter 2 8

   1. The Purpose of Dreams and Visions 8

   2. Journaling Your Dreams and Visions 9

   3. What is the Difference Between Dream, Visions and a
      Trance? 9

   4. Scriptural Examples of God Communicating Through
      Dreams and Visions 10

   5. There are Different Types of Dreams 12

Chapter 3 16

   1. Developing the Ability to Interpret Dreams and Visions 16

   2. Steps to Interpret a Dream and Vision 17

   3. A Small Dictionary of the Meaning of Colors and
      Other Items Usually Indicated in Dreams and Visions 18

Chapter 4 23

   1. Interpreting Dreams and Visions & its Spiritual Source........23

Chapter 5 28

   1. More Symbolic Meanings for Dreams and Vision.................28

   2. Biblical Understanding of Certain Terms Used For
      Dreams and Visions and Their Scriptural Examples 32

   3. Interpret Two of the Following Dreams Below and
      Analyze Them 33

Chapter 6 35

   1. Symbolic Meanings of Numbers in A Dream or Vision 35

   2. Numbers Used Symbolically Can Add More Meaning
      to Dreams And Visions: 36

   3. Another Exercise on Interpreting Dreams and Numbers.......37

Chapter 7 39

   1. When God Becomes Silent..39

Chapter 8 43

   1. 10 Exercises on Interpreting More Dreams and
      Revelations of Things 43

   2. The Meaning of the Dreams Given 45

Conclusion...57

Book Resources 59

ACKNOWLEDGMENTS

Many thanks to my Lord, Jesus Christ who has inspired me to pursue the ministry of the prophetic as a seer by way of dreams and visions and to be able to interpret my dreams and visions. He has inspired me to become a prophet to the body of Christ sometimes through singing or as a spokesman. My prophetic gift also extends to the body of Christ and to church leaders in a spirit of love and compassion, to help build their ministry spiritually as the Holy Spirit leads me.

I appreciate the years of prophetic study as a correspondent student of Pro. Dr. Bill Hamon, founder of the Christian International Theology Institute in Santa Rosa Beach, FL for four years. Before studying under Bill Hamon, I studied under the ministry of Pro. John Paul Jackson (deceased in 2015) on the ability to interpret dreams and visions for about 3 years. His ministry is entitled, "The Streams Ministry" in the state of TX.

Many thanks for the tutelage of Pro. Paulette Polo instructor at the Bethel Supernatural Ministries for two years in Cranford, N.J. Many thanks to the Kingdom Institute where I sat under Rev. Gary Fishman in a few workshops on Dream Interpretation in Cranford, N.J. It was a wonderful experience for about one or two years.

And now, I have completed my studies in dreams and visions with interpretation at the Naioth Prophetical Arts Institute where Pro. Teresa Gripper is the founder and instructor in Brooklyn, N.Y. I took another course under her on the prophetic development of a seer. Many thanks to Pro. Teresa Gripper for the added practice to have a more intimate communication with God during my devotional times with Him, and when I am interpreting dreams with the knowledge and divine guidance of the Holy Spirit to be able to discern the full meaning of the dreams.

COMPLIMENTS

Rev. Sandra Washington is an amazing phenomenal woman. Her desire to pursue a deeper understanding of God's voice and wisdom within the Prophetic is exceptional. She has mastered the letter (study) of Prophecy and aims to perfect the Spiritual dimensions, especially in the area of understanding dreams and visions. She is a student par excellence, with commitment and diligence. She is apt to share whatever she has learned with everyone. She is an asset to the Kingdom of God. Prophet Teresa Gripper, CEO & Instructor at the Naioth Prophetical Arts Institute, Brooklyn, N.Y.

Dear Rev. Washington, thank you for introducing me to such an awesome class on Understanding the Dreams you Dream. From this class, I realize that God speaks to us in various ways especially through dreams. It is important to interpret those dreams. As we do so, it is important to keep a diary of them. As I continue to learn more, I am mindful that the focus of all dreams is the giver of all dreams, Jesus Christ who wants to relate to us. Chaplain Ethel Pettway, student

I've always wondered how people are able to correctly interpret dreams and visions. By taking the class, "Dreams and Visions" with Rev. Sandra Washington, I learned you need to write the dream down as much as you can remember, then you should focus on what the "main focus" of the dream was, what the sub focus was and the details. We need to use a reliable dream dictionary that is Biblically based to help interpret the dream or vision and then rely on the Holy Spirit to reveal the total meaning of the dream or vision.

I am glad I took the course because now I am able to understand dreams and visions much better and interpret not only my own, but the dreams of others as well. Rev. Edith P. Lazenby, student & writer/author.

THE INTRODUCTION

It is my desire to share with the body of Christ and with unbelievers, God's love and desire to communicate with them, especially through dreams and visions. Sometimes God may communicate with the unbelievers by way of dreams and visions as a way of introducing Himself to them, as well as, to stir them up to accept Him, or to get their attention and instill in them the invitation and need to receive salvation, through the acceptance of His Son, Jesus Christ. This is what happened and still is happening to thousands of Muslims who were brought up in the Islamic religion. They either had an open vision encounter with Jesus Christ, dreamed about Jesus Christ meeting them and encouraging them to come to Him, or read about Him in the Holy Bible and compared it with the Koran doctrine. They found out in the Holy Bible that Jesus Christ is God and that He is love with compassion. As a result, thousands of Muslims have accepted the Christian faith, especially in the Middle East nations.

Today, Muslims that were once of the Islamic faith are now suffering persecution by their own families and Islamic friends because of their belief in Jesus Christ. In the Islamic faith, Satan has blinded their eyes, as well as the eyes of the unbelievers, spiritually speaking from the one and true light of God through Jesus Christ. Those Muslims and unbelievers who have accepted Jesus Christ as their personal Savior have realized that He is the true door to the true and living God by way of the Holy Spirit and that God is the true God who made and created them as well as everything in the universe and on earth.

This dreams and visions handbook is addressed to anyone who wishes to know how God speaks to them, especially through dreams and visions. It is specifically addressed to Christians who have the indwelling of the Holy Spirit that they received through the acceptance of Jesus Christ. This handbook was written to help them to understand the mysteries of God's messages in the dreams and visions revealed to them. The best time God can speak to us is when we are still in a state of slumber when we are not busy and our minds are not cluttered with the cares of this world. This is the simplest way for God to communicate with people who are active and that is when they are still in a deep sleep.

The highest level of God communicating with us is when we are in our waking state. In this case, one definitely needs to have a relationship with Jesus Christ by way of the Holy Spirit. This is when we as believers in Christ need to learn and practice how to hear God as well as read the word of God concerning his character and deeds, so we can recognize Christ's voice speaking to us. God wants so much to communicate with us so He can share His secrets with us that would build us up spiritually so that He can help us reach our destiny according to His will.

In this handbook, you will learn the purposes as to why God speaks through dreams and visions. You will also know the difference between dreams and visions, learn the meaning of symbols of objects, colors, numbers and persons in dreams and how to use them to interpret dreams and visions with the help of the Holy Spirit. After your symbolic research, the Holy Spirit will give you an impression or a revelatory meaning of the dream or vision when you ask Him for the meaning. This is so that we would understand what God is relaying to us either to give us direction for our lives, protection or even a warning to put us back on the path of righteousness.

You will also learn the difference between Head Knowledge and Revelation Knowledge and that God Reveals his secret messages in various ways.

It is hoped that you will be blessed and inspired to seek and expect God to communicate with you and you with Him through visions and dreams, as well as in your waking state. He speaks to you by way of a still small voice, by an impression, or in a song or riddle. There will be exercises in this area along with the ability or skill to interpret dreams and visions.

CHAPTER 1

WHAT IS REVELATION KNOWLEDGE AND HEAD KNOWLEDGE?

Head knowledge is what you acquire through life's experiences, knowledge you have gained through getting an education, that is, what you have learned from books, from the Bible and from other literature and knowledge taught by parents when you were a child in order to function in this physical world.

Revelation knowledge is what the Holy Spirit reveals to a believer spiritual knowledge of God or Jesus Christ to his or her redeemed human spirit in order for his or her faith to develop to trust God to manifest His to answers one's prayers and expect His Promises. 1Corinthians 2: 9,10 (MEV), "But as it is written: Eye has not seen nor ear heard nor has it entered into the heart of man the things which God has prepared for those who love Him". "But God has revealed them to us by His Spirit. For the Spirit searches all things, yes, the deep things of God".

God gives us revelation knowledge through the various ways: He speaks to believers in Christ and to unbelievers even though unbelievers are blind to the Spirit of God who is responsible of them having intuition or having a six sense. They can only be aware of God's voice is when they give their lives to Jesus Christ as they accept Him as their Savior for the pardoning of their sins. It is the task of the Holy Spirit to reveal things to come to us Christians stated in John 16:13 (MEV), it says, "But when the Spirit of Truth comes, He (the Holy Spirit) will guide you into all truth.

For He will not speak on His own authority, but He will speak whatever He hears (from God and Jesus Christ) and He will tell you things that are to come.

He reveals God's secrets to us when He speaks to us via a still small voice, via an impression or an unction within the believer or feeling in the believer's spirit that won't go away or via a spontaneous thought or idea that was not there in ones mind. The idea or thought suddenly appeared in one's mind making sure that the thought that comes to mind lines up with the Word of God and is of God's character as well as it benefits you and mankind. God can speak through circumstances like for the purpose of correction and character development.

He can speak to us through a preached word by any one of the fivefold ministers or through prophecy given by any Christian believer or prophecy given by a child who is brought up in the admonition of God's word taught by his parents. God can also speak through His written Word in the Holy Bible when we as Christian read and apply His written in our life's situations and get to know Him through His written word.

Through the Baptism in the Holy Spirit which is receiving more of God's presence within a believer upon request and is subsequently received after salvation through Jesus Christ, God can speak by way of the spiritual gifts of the Holy Spirit. There are 9 gifts listed in the Bible in 1Corinthians 12: 1-11. They are as follows:

THE REVELATORY GIFTS OR MANIFESTATIONS OF THE HOLY SPIRIT THAT KNOWS SOMETHING

THE WORD OF KNOWLEDGE: The word of knowledge is a supernatural manifestation of the Holy Spirit revealing to a Spirit-filled believer in Christ facts about a person, place or thing concerning its past or present state. It can be revealed through dreams and visions, perceived through an impression or by a still small voice at waking state of the believer.

THE WORD OF WISDOM: The word of wisdom is a supernatural manifestation of the Holy Spirit revealing to a Spirit=filled believer God's plan and purpose of a person, place or thing concerning its future destiny in life. God can also reveal the word of wisdom of how to solve a problem without anyone telling the believer how to solve the problem. God gives the believer wisdom how to solve a particular problem. God also can reveal a Word of Wisdom of how to keep from getting entrapped by an accuser or in a situation. The word of wisdom can be revealed through dreams and visions, by a still small voice or by an inward knowing or intuition.

THE GIFT OF DISCERNING OF SPIRITS: The gift of discerning of spirits is a supernatural manifestation of the Holy Spirit revealing to a Spirit-filled believer activities happening in the spirit realm only. The believer is given the ability to see, sense, hear, and smell what is going on the spirit realm, such as, demon spirits, angelic spirits, sense Jesus Christ's presence and hear His voice, Satan's presence and hearing his voice, determine a doctrine to be not of God even though it may appear to be said with good intentions or motives. This gift is usually operated by seer prophets; however, every believer should have this gift of discerning of spirits so that they can perceive what spirit is operating in a person, place or thing and whether their motives are godly or evil; to determine whether something is done deliberately or accidentally by human error. This does not mean a believer should assume he is using the gift to judge people or a thing having a demon The believer is to rely on the Holy Spirit only to reveal to him or her the type of spirit operating within a person, place or thing so that the believer should be able to judge people rightly by the Holy Spirit. The gift of discerning of spirits can be revealed by way of dreams and visions, and through the use of spiritual senses of a believer.

THE UTTERANCE SPIRITUAL GIFTS OR GIFTS THAT SAY SOMETHING

THE GIFT OF PROPHECY: The gift of prophecy is a supernatural manifestation of the Holy Spirit through a Spirit-filled believer in Christ an inspired word of God expressing His love and care as God edifies, comforts and exhort or encourages the recipient. Prophecy can be revealed through prophets (if called by God to be a Prophet) and believers can prophesy who are filled with Christ's Spirit or the Holy Spirit. Prophecy can be revealed by a still small voice and by dreams and visions. Prophecy can have a futuristic message from God when the word of wisdom of God is in conjunction with it. There are prophecies that forth tell, that is, prophecies that are inspired messages from God that edify, comfort and exhort at the moment to a recipient and there are prophecies that foretell, that is, there are prophecies that are futuristic or prophetic that tells God's plan and purpose for the future of a person, place or thing.

THE GIFT OF DIVERSE TONGUES: The gift of diverse tongues is a supernatural manifestation of the Holy Spirit through a Spirit-filled believer in Christ of an inspired message in a heavenly language or tongues to a person, congregation in a church or to a group of people. The believer speaks in a heavenly language like a trumpet for everyone to hear. In order for the congregation or group or person to understand what was said in tongues, the supernatural gift of Interpretation must follow either by the believer who gave God's message in tongues or someone in the congregation who is sensitive to the Holy Spirit can give the interpretation of the message in tongues. Sometimes, the message in tongues can be understood by a person in the congregation or group who can speak and understand the language as his or her native language. If the interpretation is of the message in tongues is understood by the recipients and it was edifying, comforting and exhorting or encouraging, then the message in tongues with the gift of interpretation was prophecy. This gift of diverse tongues is not the same as the devotional tongues of believers who are baptized with the Holy Spirit. In this case, the believers are praying in their prayer language unto God alone only God can understand. It is a prayer language inspired by the Holy Spirit within the believers as they pray in tongues perfect prayers to God, praying out God's mysteries perhaps concerning each believer's life, or God's plans for a nation, etc.

THE GIFT OF INTERPRETATION: The gift of interpretation is a supernatural manifestation of the holy Spirit through a Spirit-filled believer in Christ that reveals the general meaning of the inspired message spoken in diverse tongues. The gift of interpretation does not translate word for word the message in tongues. It just gives the general meaning of the message in tongues.

Again, the gift of interpretation can be spoken like a trumpet with a loud voice of the believer who gave the message in diverse tongues to a person, group or church congregation inspired by the Holy Spirit. Or the gift of interpretation can be manifested through any believer in the congregation who is spirit-filled and sensitive to the Holy Spirit to give the interpretation in English or in the native tongue in a person living in a foreign country. If the Interpretation of the message in tongues is edifying, comforting, and exhorting or encouraging, then the message is given as prophecy.

The Holy Spirit reveals God speaking to you by what God does through His power gifts:

THE POWER GIFTS OR MANIFESTATION OF THE POWER OF THE HOLY SPIRIT THAT DOES SOMETHING

THE GIFT OF FAITH: The gift of faith is the supernatural manifestation of God's faith that is not human faith nor saving faith, but God's faith given to a spirit-filled believer in Christ to expect God to do the impossible without a doubt or unbelief. God's faith is added to the saving faith (that one receives at salvation) of a believer to expect God to do what

He said He would do or say through revelation knowledge. This power gift operates in conjunction with all the spiritual gifts, but especially with the Gifts of Healings and the Gift of Working of Miracles.

THE GIFTS OF HEALINGS: The gifts of healings is the supernatural manifestation of the ability of God to restore the recipient's body from sickness and disease either through the lay-on of hands of any spirit-filled believer in Christ or an ordained minister of healing or speaking to the illness for it to leave the body by the power of the Holy Spirit. The Word of Knowledge, gift of faith, word of wisdom and the gift of discerning of spirits are generally operating in conjunction with the gifts of healings. Gifts of Healings mean that God heals in various ways for different kinds of illnesses by the direction of the Holy Spirit. Results through the gifts of healings are usually instant. Healing by faith without the direction of the Holy Spirit of how to heal the recipient is usually gradual. Healing by faith the result is gradual; however, healing eventually comes, It is a healing process. Mark 16:18; James 5:14,15.

THE GIFT OF WORKING OF MIRACLES: The gift of working of miracles is a supernatural manifestation of God's power by the Holy Spirit through any spirit-filled believer in Christ or through an ordained minister who is sensitive to God's voice telling him or her to make a command to grow out a missing part of the body of a recipient, such as growing a finger, or foot, or an arm; to cast out a demon in a person (you need the gift of discerning of spirits in operation); to control the weather, etc. This gift of miracles God operates intervenes with the course of nature and time frame of something that takes to be healed or before a disaster happens. All are performed through the believer with expectation, without a doubt by God's gift of faith operating in him or her. God's gift of miracles was operating through Moses when he was told by God to use his rod open the Red Sea. You need the gift of faith in conjunction with all of the spiritual gifts; but, again, with especially, the gifts of healings and the gift of working of miracles.

The Holy Spirit is the revelator who reveals to every Christian God and Jesus Christ's prophecies through various ways of communication and in conjunction with the nine Spiritual Gifts of the Holy Spirit. And lastly, God can reveal inspired knowledge through dreams and visions as well as trances. This handbook, "The Handbook For Understanding Your Dreams and Interpreting Them", will be emphasizing how to interpret dreams and visions for interested readers who seek to have intimacy with God and desire for Him to communicate with them His secrets about their lives, nations, about situations giving them hope, etc. through dreams and visions.

As you can see, revelatory knowledge encompasses various ways God reveals His prophetic messages within us and outside of us even in what He has created in nature. It is hoped you will be blessed by this handbook knowing how to interpret your dreams and visions and experience God's intimacy to want to communicate with you personally.

CHAPTER 2

THE PURPOSE OF DREAMS AND VISIONS

The purpose of dreams and visions is that God wants to have a close relationship with you and communicate with you so He can share His mysteries or secrets of things to come for your life, for a family member, for your community, for your nation and for other nations. This is why believers should not take their dreams for granted; but should take some time to search out the meaning of what God is saying to you whenever you dream or have a vision given by the Holy Spirit.

Even non-believers have dreams and visions. It is God's way of stimulating their appetite to search for Him and inspire them to seek out the meaning of the dream or vision if the dream and vision leaves an impression within his or her human spirit. According to Job 33:14, 15 (NASed.) it says, "Indeed God speaks once or twice, yet no one notices it in a dream, a vision of the night when sound sleep falls on men (non-believers and believers) while they slumber in their beds." Even though men may not regard dreams or visions nor take them seriously, God still reveals His will. If men do not take heed to what God is revealing to them, God will speak to them in a dream again, but in a different way in order to get His will of His message across to them.

In Job 33:16 (NAS ed.) it says, "Then He opens the ears of men and seals their instruction." In Numbers 12:6, the scripture is addressed to those whom God has called into the prophetic ministry. God says He will make Himself known to the prophets in a vision and speak to him or her in a dream. Both scriptures indicate how much God desires to communicate with His people through visions and dreams. To disregard them is to dishonor God and His love to direct the lives of His people.

JOURNALING YOUR DREAMS AND VISIONS

It is important to journal or write down in a notebook or diary the dreams and visions you remember. Those dreams or visions you do not remember, are generally not important. Only the dreams and visions that leave an impression or are engraved in your spirit so that you can never forget them for the rest of your life are the ones that count. Those types of dreams and visions are what God is using to get your attention, especially if they are repetitive. Those dreams should searched out by you, using dream dictionaries that somewhat have the meaning of certain names of images God uses in your dreams that are biblically based. Then, after your research, pray and ask the Holy Spirit for understanding of the dream. Sometimes, you may automatically know what the dream or vision means to you and what God is saying.

When you actually take the time to search out the meaning of the dream or vision, you are honoring God and respecting Him for what He is trying to reveal to you to give you direction for your life or to show you things to come for your protection. It is important that you keep a record of the dream and its meaning, indicating the date and time you received the revelation. Habakkuk 2:2(a) (Amp. ed) says, "Write the vision and engrave it plainly upon tablets."

WHAT IS THE DIFFERENCE BETWEEN DREAM, VISIONS AND A TRANCE?

1. Define a **"Dream"** – A dream is defined as a spiritual message revealed to a person when he or she is in a deep sleep. It is revealed in the form of pictures. Each dream has a symbolic

content meaning, that it must be searched and interpreted with the help of the Holy Spirit. Another definition of a dream is to have a thought or a series of thoughts, ideas or images in the mind during sleep. When sleeping, dreams are revealed as impressions on the mind of a person made by divine intrusion.

2. Define a **"Vision"** – The definition of a vision is usually revealed to a person who may be in a state of twilight sleep (or half sleep) or in a waking state when a flash of images or pictures are seen in the spirit. Visions revealed when one is half sleep is called an inward vision. Visions revealed when the person's eyes are open are called open visions or outward visions. Sometimes, a vision can be revealed in the believer's mind and spirit or it can be perceived without seeing the vision outwardly. It is more of an inward perception in a waking state. Visionary revelation is manifested in three ways: through visions, trances and dreams.

3. Define **"Trance"** - It is the surge of the Holy Spirit that causes the spirit of the Christian to experience another heavenly realm of the spirit fixating his focus on a vision sometimes accompanied with the voice of God speaking to him with his eyes open or in a half sleeping state making him unaware of his surroundings.

SCRIPTURAL EXAMPLES OF GOD COMMUNICATING THROUGH DREAMS AND VISIONS

Some Scripture examples of how God communicated to prophets and to other characters in the Bible. They are as follows:

A) Revealed God's Promises:

1. Genesis 37:5-10; Joseph's dream from God of his future leadership position.

2. Isaiah 45:1-7- God uses the heathen Cyrus as His anointed to save His people Israel from the Babylonian captivity.

B) God gives direction:

1. Matthew 1:20- Joseph was told that Mary was pregnant by the Holy Spirit.
2. Acts 9:10 - Ananias was told to restore Saul. God would use Saul for a purpose.
3. Acts 16:9- Paul had a vision of a man asking to minister in Macedonia.

C) Warning Dreams and Visions:

1. Matthew 2:13 – Joseph was warned to take Mary and Jesus to Egypt for safety.
2. Genesis 41:14 – 37 – Joseph interprets Pharoah's dream that warned of an upcoming years of plenty followed by a famine.
3. Matthew 2:12 – Wise men warned not to return to Herod.

D) Dreams used to predict future events:

1. Daniel 2:31-45 – Daniel interprets Nebuchadnezzar's dream of future Gentile Empires that will take Israel captive.
2. The whole book of Revelation starting from chapter 6 – Apostle John is given an open vision of Christ depicting what will happen in the future of the unbelievers and the Orthodox Jews.

E) Dreams used to give courage:

1. Acts 18:9,10 - Paul was encouraged in a vision that he will not be harmed in Corinth when sharing the gospel of Jesus Christ.
2. Acts 27:23 – Paul had an open vision of an angel during a shipwreck.

F) There are minor prophets that God did not communicate through dreams nor visions: Hosea, Joel, Obadiah, Jonah, Micah, Nahum, Habakkuk, Zephaniah, Haggai and Malachai.

THERE ARE DIFFERENT TYPES OF DREAMS

There are twenty categories of dreams. They are as follows:

1. **Healing Dreams** - It could be dreams that can heal relationships; change an attitude toward people, or inspire forgiveness or physical healing.

2. **Flushing Dreams** - Revealing a process of deliverance or cleansing of lustful tendencies and is washed away within the dreamer; if the person is observing, it deals with someone else being cleansed.

3. **Calling Dreams** - Provokes you to seek God for what He has called you to do. It also means to position yourself for the calling.

4. **Warning Dreams** - Judgment is coming, warning to guide you to take another way; a dream that can show you a warning of a nation or another person.

5. **False Dreams** - Whatever the enemy is doing to you in the dream, do not accept it in your waking state. It is because God is going to do something opposite to what the devil showed you in the dream concerning your destiny, for example.

6. **Body Dreams** - Usually your body is going through a transition; it comes by a physical condition. Sometimes the dream can be literal or symbolic.

7. **Chemical Dreams** - Instigated by certain medications that can cause a person to have nightmares. One must pray against this type of dream.

8. **Self-Condition or Self-Evaluation Dream** - a dream that exposes where you stand with God; where your maturation process is with God; tells what needs to change in your life in order to reach the destiny that God plans for your life.

9. **Courage Dreams** - Such dreams help to build you up with courage, strengthens faith to do what God calls you to do.

10. **Correction Dreams** – Such a dream deals with your attitude towards something or someone; cause your opinions to change; reveals an error you may have made and God is revealing a correction.

11. **Direction Dreams** - God giving direction as to how to achieve a calling, and how to reach your destiny; He can give direction as to how to solve a problem.

12. **Intercession Dreams** – God may reveal to you a person to pray for or a nation or leader to pray for. In waking state, you are to pray for that same thing.

13. **Prophecy and Revelation Dreams** - A dream that reveals the future or the word of wisdom and other revelation gifts of the Holy Spirit. For example, God can give you a dream of a word of knowledge on how to heal a specific illness or give you a dream of the gift of discerning of spirits detecting a demon causing an illness, etc.

14. **Dark Dreams** - Dark shadows, black and white or muted dreams are usually from the enemy of what he is doing in the spirit realm. If it is black and white, depicts deception; the demonic. If

the dream was from God, it would be in color. In Dark Dreams, Satan is trying to stop you from achieving God's goals for your life or calling. This is when you have to take authority over Satan's plans and schemes.

15. **Spiritual Warfare Dreams** - Such dreams are usually dark, black and white, and dark colors. In such a dream, Satan attacks you or sometimes God allows you to see what Satan is doing in the spirit realm. In waking state this is when you need to war against what the enemy is doing with the help of the Holy Spirit, requesting God to send His angels to fight on your behalf and to protect you as you plead the blood of Jesus over your life and family.

16. **Fear Dreams** - Outward and Inward fears can cause you to dream fearful dreams and have nightmares. It is a soul dream. What you fear you empower. You need to pray against fear and take authority over it using the word of God. For God has not given us a spirit of fear, but of love, power and of a sound mind.

17. **Invention Dreams**-This dream shares creative ideas that come from God; it gives you solutions for things to invent; create a song; create art, etc.

18. **Word of Knowledge Dreams** - Gives divine knowledge concerning a person, place or thing. Dreams that give you solutions to solve a problem, insight and understanding in dealing with God's agenda or plan.

19. **Deliverance Dreams** - The Lord intervenes and delivers one in the dream from the attacks of the enemy. In this dream, He may reveal the demon involved for one to cast out when ministering healing in waking state.

20. **Soul Dreams** - Are usually dark, black and white or muted dreams. Such dreams are personal desires projected in a dream. It is an expression from your soul. If of sin, one needs to repent in waking state. A sanctified soul is a soul who wishes to do God's will or to be used of God in a dream. This is a good dream.

CHAPTER 3

DEVELOPING THE ABILITY TO INTERPRET DREAMS AND VISIONS

A dream that is not understood can be disregarded or ignored, however, when understood, a dream and/or vision becomes a life changing experience. Remember the pictures in a dream can be symbolic or taken literally. They do not always mean the same thing from dream to dream.

There are two questions to answer:

1. How can believers determine what dreams or visions are from God or from the Devil?

2. Since dreams are mostly symbolic and metaphoric, how do believers interpret their meaning?

Answer for question 1: Dreams that are in color have a divine positive meaning. The meaning of the dream should be in one accord with the Word of God. Lastly, if the dream, once again, is engraved in your spirit so that it never escapes your memory, in some cases, for a life time, know that the dream comes from God by way of the Holy Spirit.

Again, black and white or muted or dark dreams that have no color nor remnants of light, are usually negative in nature or in meaning. If the dream does not line up with the Word of God, it becomes intimidating, scary, lustful, etc., and you would know that it's from the enemy. Again, the believer is to take authority using God's Word to stand against Satan in these dreams in waking state.

Answer for question 2: Again, as was said at the beginning in lesson 1, but, bears repeating, when interpreting dreams, it is good to have a dream dictionary or dictionaries beside you that are biblically interpreted. Always ask the Holy Spirit to help you to understand the meaning of the dream once you have done your research of the symbolic images in your dream and vision. It is important to journal your dreams and vision so you can reflect on them when they do come to pass. The next thing are steps to use to interpret your dreams.

STEPS TO INTERPRET A DREAM AND VISION

1. Always journal your dreams and visions.
2. Indicate the date and time of your visions and dreams
3. Determine the category of your dream, then give it a title.
4. Ask yourself the following questions:

   a) Where am I in the dream; as an observer or a participant?
   b) What or Who is the main focus? The dreamer or another character?
   c) What is or are the sub-focus (the other elements in a dream that are necessary in order to find the theme or plot that make it have meaning)? It is anything related to the focus.
   d) What are the details (extra minor images or items that add to the meaning of the dream, such as colors, clothing, objects, etc.)?
   e) Make a diagram of your dream or make an outline form to diagram your dream like the one on page 25.
   f) Now look up the symbolic images in the dream
   g) Ask the Holy Spirit to interpret the meaning of the dream after your research.

h) Ask yourself, did the meaning give you a sense of comfort and direction. If you interpret someone else's dream, ask them if it meant anything to them.

A SMALL DICTIONARY OF THE MEANING OF COLORS AND OTHER ITEMS USUALLY INDICATED IN DREAMS AND VISIONS [1]

MEANING OF COLORS

COLORS	POSITIVE	NEGATIVE
RED	Anointing, Passion, Wisdom	Anger or War
BLUE	Revelation, Peace, Communion	Depression
GREEN	Conscience, Life, Growth, Health	Envy or Pride
BROWN (ALSO TAN)	Compassion, Humility	Compromise Soulish, Flesh

COLORS	POSITIVE	NEGATIVE
Negative colors are: Muted (has no colorful figures); Black and White, darkness		
GOLD/AMBER	Purity, Majesty	Idolatry
PURPLE	Royalty, Authority, Intercession	False authority
ORANGE	Perseverance, power	Stubbornness, Witchcraft
SILVER	Redemption, Knowledge and Grace	Legalism fear, Intellectual

---

[1] Understanding Dreams and Visions Course 201; pg 137, by John Paul Jackson

YELLOW	Spiritual gifts, Hope	Pride
PINK	Child-like, love, passion	Illness, Childish in behavior or attitude
GRAY	Maturity, Honor	Compromiser, Confused
WHITE	Righteousness, Holiness, and Purity	Religious Spirit
BLACK	Creativity hidden; Secretive	Soulish, Darkness

1. **Emotions** in dreams are important. Feelings can tell a lot when interpreting dreams and visions. You can associate colors with emotions for yourself, people and creatures.
2. **Sexual Encounters** They can be satanic and they can be very intimate. It can be healthy when it comes to genuine relationships with the opposite sex.
3. **Transportation** Vehicles generally have to do with ministry or vocation

A) Vehicles:

1. **Airplane:** A ministry or business is able to go to the highest spiritual level for success.
2. **Automobile:** Personal ministry or job.
3. **Convertible:** Open heaven.
4. **Bus:** A church or ministry that has a teaching ministry.
5. **Truck:** A small or big ministry task; encouragement Semi-truck or an 18 wheeler: Partial ministry task.

   Tow Truck: A ministry of helps to gather the wounded people that hurt emotionally or physically.

   Fire Truck: A rescuer or deliverer; to purge or cleanse.

6. **Tractor:** plow the ground so that the foundation of the gospel is established.

7. **Bicycle:** The person has to work the ministry to get it where it should be spiritually and physically.
8. **Armored car:** The ministry is protected by God.
9. **Taxi cab:** To pay a price to get where your ministry is going; a hireling to be paid to do a ministry task.
10. **Stagecoach:** The ministry maybe somewhat rough and difficult to handle or to ride, however, it will eventually succeed.
11. **Rollercoaster:** The ministry will either be exciting or be a temporary thrill.
12. **Limousine:** Your ministry will be taken to its destiny by God.
13. **Train:** The ministry will have the strength and movement of God.

B) Ships/Boats:

1. **Ocean Liner:** A mega church or ministry.
2. **Tugboat:** Ministry of helps
3. **Sailboat(s):** Ministry powered by the Holy Spirit; to have influence upon the people.
4. **Riverboat:** A ministry that stimulates life like a river; it has an atmosphere of joy. It is the start of revival in the church.
5. **Speedboat:** The Holy Spirit helps a ministry to reach its goals speedily.
6. **Submarine:** Ministry is under cover, hidden; people do not recognize it.

C) Other Vehicles:

1. **Subway:** Undercover; people do not see it or recognize the ministry, a hidden ministry not well known.
2. **Helicopter:** Ministry going on a higher realm in the Spirit, it is mobile.
3. **Chariot:** A major spiritual encounter if it takes your ministry from earth to heaven.

4. **Spaceship:** Ministry full of faith; not limiting God; all things are possible.

D) Buildings:

Note the size and purpose of the building.

1. **House:** Can represent you or a church.
2. **Castle:** Authority, fortress or stronghold; where a king lives.
3. **Barn:** Provision or storage.
4. **Mall:** A marketplace, place of multiple ministries networking together, materialism, self-centeredness, shopping addiction.
5. **Stadium:** A large impact on the people.
6. **Elevator:** The rise and decrease of a spiritual level or anointing for a particular position in a dream or vision.
7. **Staircase:** Climbing upwards or downwards spiritually in ministry or in whatever God calls you to do. It can also mean portal of heaven.
8. **High rise buildings:** high spiritual calling.
9. **Hotel:** A temporary place to relax and receive fellowship with God
10. **Country general store:** Refers to basic needs or staples of life; refers to God supplying all of our needs.
11. **Amphitheater:** Something is going to be magnified.
12. **Theater:** to be shown something.
13. **Windows:** God is giving you a vision to see the future; allowing the glory of God to come.
14. **Garden:** Love, intimacy in a prayer life; tells of growth in the spirit.
15. **Front porch, front door, or front** of anything on a building, usually tells what is going to happen in the future of that person.
16. **Back porch, back door, backyard** of a house or building usually tells of what happened in the past.
17. **Hallway:** Something or Someone transitioning; can't deviate from the path you are on.

18. **Hospital:** deals with healing issues.
19. **Garage:** You or your ministry is at rest; can be a place of storage.
20. **Auto Repair Shop:** A ministry receives restoration or needs repair.
21. **Gas station:** A ministry or person that needs a refilling of the power of the Holy Spirit.
22. **Office Building:** Being in an office of a calling.
23. **Roof:** Spiritual covering
24. **Farm:** A place of growth.
25. **Airport:** Going to your spiritual destiny.

Consult other Dream dictionaries that are biblically based to get the full meaning of the items above and other dream symbols.

CHAPTER 4

INTERPRETING DREAMS AND VISIONS & ITS SPIRITUAL SOURCE

Be careful who is interpreting your dreams and by what spiritual source. Make sure you are interpreting your dreams not by the soulish realm, but by the Spirit of Jesus Christ, the Holy Spirit. Make sure your interpretation is in one accord with the Word of God and His character.

Analyze the following dream or vision examples in the format below. Use the steps stated in lesson 2 on how to interpret the dreams or visions. Determine the title, theme and category last:

The first dream has been done for you as an example on how to analyze it:

> *"In a dream, I observed a woman dressed in ordinary clothes. She was walking across a city street in the dark, however, storefront lights and lights from the street lamp posts were shining. As the woman was crossing the street, her face lit up with the glory of God. The pedestrians looked at her with awe and said, "owh.""*

Part the dreamer played:	Observer
Main Focus:	The Woman
The Sub Focus:	The face of the woman reflecting the glory of God; dark street; pedestrians in awe saying "Owh."
Details:	Lights from storefronts and street lamp posts, city.
	Dream was in color
Title:	The Awakening of the Church
Symbolic Meaning	Research Symbols
Category:	A Prophetic dream for the dreamer and church body

Interpretation of Symbols: Dark City = Blind or confused condition of the general public of unbelievers, or Apostate church.

The Woman dressed in ordinary clothing = represents a spirit- filled Church or an anointed Christian; lights coming from the lamp posts = the word of God lighting the path of one's life; lights from the storefronts = a chain of ministries filled with the Holy Spirit; woman crossing the street in the dark = during her spiritual journey in the midst of a crisis or trial or sinful circumstances; woman reflected with God's glory on her face = the individual or the remnant church will shine with God's glory doing the works of Christ by the anointing of the Holy Spirit; People gaze at the woman with awe saying "Owh" = The people representing the city or even nations or all humanity will gaze at the glory of God upon the remnant church or individual Christians all over the world doing the works of Jesus Christ. People being drawn to her light.

Meaning of the Dream Directed by the Holy Spirit: This dream is a prophetic dream depicting another move of God's glory coming to earth by way of the Holy Spirit that will awaken and come upon the body of

Christ in the last days during the time of crisis in our cities or nation(s). The body of Christ will be anointed to do the works of Christ; to be of help to people who are still walking in confusion, sickness, and living immorally. This dream reminds one of Isaiah 60:1-5 that will come to pass.

Analyze and Interpret two more dreams according to the example above:

1. *"I observed a gold chain with a padlock that had a ruby in the center of it." (check your dream answer on page 52).*

What is the dreamer doing?: *(Observing or Participating)*	
Main Focus:	
Sub Focus:	
Detail(s): *(Includes color, muted, Black and White, darkness, light, etc.)*	
Title:	
Category:	
Interpret or research the symbolic words:	
What does the dream mean? *(Consult the Holy Spirit)*	

2. *"In the 1990's while studying for the ministry in Tulsa, OK. I observed the animation of Jesus Christ's head outlined in blue sky. The sky was full of little pieces of hail. Jesus blew wind on the pieces of hail. The hails turned into fiery stars in the heavens."* If you have had dreams and visions, take the time to practice interpreting them according to the steps mentioned in **chapter 3.** *(check your dream answer on page 52).*

What is the dreamer doing?: (Observing or Participating)	
Main Focus:	
Sub Focus:	
Detail(s): (Includes color, muted, Black and White, darkness, light, etc.)	
Title:	
Category:	
Interpret or research the symbolic words:	
What does the dream mean? (Consult the Holy Spirit)	

Write the dream on another writing pad and analyze it in the format stated above.

PRACTICE JOURNALING AND HEARING THE VOICE OF GOD

You would need a notebook or writing pad and pen:

The following images are given for you to imagine. Pray in the Spirit first (speak in tongues) or take a few moments to stir up your spirit through worshipping the Lord. Then ask the Holy Spirit to use the images of objects given to you below to give you a spiritual message concerning those images. Then, ask the Holy Spirit to expand the message further by revealing more revelatory usage of the word images given. Suggested images given are as follows:

1. Eagle; 2. An ocean; 3. White pearls; 4. A water fall; 5. Yellow rose

2. Write a journal of the messages God speaks to you of for each image stated above.

3. Ask the Holy Spirit to give you an image. Ask Him what the image means to you. Write below what the image means to you. Write down the message that the Holy Spirit gives.

CHAPTER 5

MORE SYMBOLIC MEANINGS FOR DREAMS AND VISION

A) Objects or implements:

1. **Knife:** Knife can mean a verbal attack, negative gossip or any other communicative issue.
2. **Sword:** The word of God, verbal influence
3. **Gun:** Spiritual authority; verbal attacks
4. **Dart:** Curses or demonic attacks
5. **Ring:** Covenant or authority

B) Clothing: Anointed covering of God; depending on the colors.

1. **Coat:** Covered with the anointing of God (depending on the color of the coat).
2. **Swimwear:** Revealing deeper things of the Spirit.
3. **Hat:** A called position; or a covering of the Holy Spirit
4. **Wedding dress:** Having a deep relationship or covenant with someone personally or with Jesus Christ, the Bridegroom.
5. **Shoes:** Peace, good news, taking the gospel to others (depending on the color of the shoes).
6. **Clothing that does not fit:** Walking in something you are not called into or anointed for.

C) Creatures:

1. **Snake:** Demonic; a long tale or a lie
   White snake: A spirit of religion or a religious lie
2. **Horse:** Power, movement of God (depending on the color of the Horse).
3. **Ox/cow:** Slow change, provision or food (depending on the circumstance).
4. **Rat:** Sin issues that need to be taken care of.
5. **Spider:** Deals with witchcraft; web means trap
6. **Butterfly:** Transforming into a different person
7. **Bee/hornet:** painful; strong demonic attack against an anointed person.
8. **Flies:** Live off of dead things; full of lies
9. **Wolves:** false authority or false teaching (wolves in sheep clothing).
10. **Frog:** spirit of lust
11. **Monkey:** mockery; addiction
12. **Black panther:** high level witchcraft; occult activity
13. **Sheep:** Humility or submission; sacrifice; people of God; prosperity.
14. **Goat:** The unrighteous; blessings or abundance.
15. **Donkey:** Burden bearer; of gentle strength; can be stubborn
16. **Tiger:** Stubborn soul issues; soul power.
17. **Octopus:** Jezebel spirit.
18. **Alligator (or Crocodile):** gossip or one who has a big mouth.
19. **Elephant:** A big issue that needs tending; one who is aggressive after the things in the Spirit.
20. **Whale:** Emphasizing things of the Spirit
21. **Bear:** Judgment; strength
22. **Cat:** The will; having an independent thinking; **Black cat:** Witchcraft.
23. **Mule:** Having a stubborn nature
24. **Eagle:** A prophetic calling

25. **Hawk:** An intercessory call in the prophetic
26. **Turtle:** Tender hearted; yet has strength
27. **Dogs:** Generational curse; can be a loyal friend (depending on the colors of the dogs and their emotions towards a person in the dream)
28. **Rabbits:** Something multiplying quickly.

D) Weather Images:

1. **Storms:** White storms are from God; dark or black storms are from the enemy.
2. **Clouds:** White clouds are from God; dark, gray overcast=a storm coming, or judgment.
3. **Tornadoes:** White tornadoes are from God; dark tornadoes are from the enemy; trouble ahead.
4. **Wind:** Holy Spirit; trouble ahead (if wind is dark and very windy)
5. **Rain:** if clear it represents the Holy Spirit; if dark, it represents the enemy or trouble on the way.
6. **Earthquake:** Judgment or a shaking coming (good or bad).
7. **Snow:** Favor, righteousness; a refreshing.

E) Rooms in a house:

1. **Bathroom:** cleansing or flushing the soulish spirit
2. **Bathroom in full view:** cleansing exposed
3. **Kitchen:** heart issues; preparing and eating spiritual food as preparation to teach
4. **Restaurant kitchen:** affecting more people teaching the Word of God.
5. **Dining Room/eating:** partaking of the teaching or fellowship
6. **Attic:** History or past issues
7. **Basement:** Hidden issues; issues under the surface.
8. **Bedroom:** intimacy, a place of rest.
9. **Living room:** relationships and public relations.

F) Body Parts:

1. **Thigh:** Faith, covenant, core of your strength.
2. **Nose:** Discernment, to tell of something.
3. **Hand:** Relationship or giving direction or represent the fivefold ministry
4. **Arm:** Faith, strength
5. **Teeth:** wisdom and understanding
6. **Eye teeth:** Revelatory understanding
7. **Wisdom teeth:** Ability to understand wisdom
8. **Immobilization of body parts:** demonic attack or demonic visitation
9. **Beard:** Maturity
10. **Hair:** Wisdom or anointing.
11. **Nakedness:** Transparency; humility without guile; nothing hidden.
12. **Neck:** Will, stubborn, stiff necked.
13. **Side of body:** A place of friendship or relationship or Vulnerability.
14. **Ankle:** The ability to walk out the call of God.
15. **Money:** Favor; money lost: lost favor; Black and White money: Greed.
16. **Repeated Activities:** God repeats something you haven't settled yet

G) Miscellaneous symbols:

1. **Trees:** Leaders of nations, people, leaders of churches, and purposes of leaders depending on type of trees (oak, maple, evergreen, etc.)
2. **Flying:** The ability to go over life's circumstances; have a prophetic ministry or anointing.
3. **Left:** Destined to do, born to do, or a spiritual direction
4. **Right:** Divine faith or strength to do something
5. **Pool or Lakes:** Represents a church; people in the community.
6. **Waterfall:** Move of the Holy Spirit.

BIBLICAL UNDERSTANDING OF CERTAIN TERMS USED FOR DREAMS AND VISIONS AND THEIR SCRIPTURAL EXAMPLES [2]

1. Dreams

A) In the Old Testament (using Hebrew words)

1. Chalem: means dream in Hebrew (Daniel 2:4-6; 4:18-19)
2. Challam: A dream that reveals the destiny of the dreamer or gives strategic ways to win a battle. (Gen. 37:5; 40:5; Judges 7:13)

B) In the New Testament (using Hebrew words)

1. Onar: A dream (Matt. 2: 13, 19, 22; 27: 19)
2. Enupnion: Dreams given to people throughout the world (Acts 2:17,18); dreams that warn people of their lifestyle (Jude 1:8).

2. Visions

A) Old Testament (in Hebrew)

1. Machezeh: A vision; the word of the Lord comes in a vision (Gen. 15:1; Numbers 24: 4,16)
2. Chazah: A dream, a revelation, sight, vision (Ps. 89:19; Prov.29:18; Daniel 8:2; Isaiah 1:1)
3. Mareh/Marah: seeing, appearance, sight or image (Ezek. 1:1; 8:3,4; 11:24; Daniel 8: 26; 10:8).
4. Ra'ah: To see, vision, look upon (2 Chron. 26: 5)
5. Ra'eh: A vision or a seer (1 Samuel 9:9; Isaiah 28:7)

---

[2] Ibid pgs 13 – 17 by John Paul Jackson

B) New Testament

1. Optasia: An apparition, a sigh at, vision or open vision (Luke 24: 23; Acts 26: 19; 2 Cor. 12: 1).
2. Horama: Something gazed at, a sight, a thing seen, vision, open vision. (Acts 9:10, 12; 10:3, 18:9)
3. Horasis: A sign, an appearance, seeing, open vision (Revelation 9:17; Acts 2:17)

INTERPRET TWO OF THE FOLLOWING DREAMS BELOW AND ANALYZE THEM

1. *The dreamer dreamed of the U.S.A. all green on a colorful map. The U.S.A. was displaced from its normal place on the map and placed within Saudi Arabia in the Middle East on the map (Interpret the dream). (check your dream answer on page 53).*

What is the dreamer doing?: *(Observing or Participating)*	
Main Focus:	
Sub Focus:	
Detail(s): *(Includes color, muted, Black and White, darkness, light, etc.)*	
Title:	
Category:	
Interpret or research the symbolic words:	
What does the dream mean? *(Consult the Holy Spirit)*	

2. *The dreamer dreamed of U.S.A. again on a globe suspended in the atmosphere of the blue universe. This time all of America on the globe was all black. Outlining the shape of America were small cars moving slowly around the shape of America. Each car was lit up with the amber color of the glory of God or the Holy Spirit (interpret the dream). (check your dream answer on page 54).*

What is the dreamer doing?: *(Observing or Participating)*	
Main Focus:	
Sub Focus:	
Detail(s): *(Includes color, muted, Black and White, darkness, light, etc.)*	
Title:	
Category:	
Interpret or research the symbolic words:	
What does the dream mean? *(Consult the Holy Spirit)*	

CHAPTER 6

SYMBOLIC MEANINGS OF NUMBERS
IN A DREAM OR VISION

Sometimes God uses numbers in dreams and visions literally, figuratively and symbolically. An example of numbers used literally can be in dreams or visions to describe a date, a year or a scripture. In a dream, God showed me 1806 against a circular azure blue color. I actually knew God was referring to the year of 1806. The azure blue color is symbolic of the Holy Spirit and peace. I was curious and started doing some research as to what happened in 1806 spiritually. I found out during 1806 a small revival or a spiritual awakening started on a college campus in Boston, Mass. called the Haystack Revival in which a group of college students got together in a stable and took delight worshipping the Lord and receiving the baptism in the Holy Spirit after they received salvation. I believe through the mini dream of 1806, God was telling me that a revival will come to our nation, America. A move of the Holy Spirit awakening is coming to our nation. Also refer to Revelations 11:3, notice the number 1260 is a literal number, describing the number of days the two witnesses will be ministering during the last half of the Great Tribulation.

Numbers used literary, or figuratively, poetically in a story form or in a parable form, can give a dream special meaning and understanding to the theme of the dream or vision. For example, In Matthew 24:31, the number 4 is used figuratively, "And He will send His angels with a great sound of a trumpet, and they will gather together His elect from the four winds, from one end of heaven to the other. Four represents the four corners of the earth.

In Genesis 41:17-31, the number 7 is used figuratively to mean something positive or negative. In this passage of scripture, Joseph interprets the dream of Pharaoh who had two dreams with the same meaning. In one dream, he dreamed of 7 healthy cows being eaten up by 7 ugly thin cows and in the second dream, 7 healthy ears of corn were eaten up by the thin ears of corn that were damaged by the heat of the wind. In the first dream, 7 represented 7 years of plenty. In the second dream, 7 represented 7 years of famine.

NUMBERS USED SYMBOLICALLY CAN ADD MORE MEANING TO DREAMS AND VISIONS: [3]

1	=	God, beginning, unity and importance (Gen. 1: 1,5b)
2	=	witness, divided, discerning (Gen. 1: 6,8)
3	=	likeness, trinity, conform (Matt. 28:19)
4	=	Reign, rule (over the world), kingdom, world, creation (Gen. 1:16,18,19)
5	=	To serve, grace, service, atonement (Gen. 41:34; Eph. 4:11)
6	=	Image, humanity, man; fleshy, carnal, idol, Satan (Rev. 13:18; Gen. 1: 26)
7	=	Completion, finished, rest (Gen. 2:1, 3)
8	=	New beginnings, put on the new man, take off the old man (Col. 3: 9; 1Peter 3:20); to sanctify (2 Chron. 29:17)
9	=	Being fruitful, harvest; (Gal. 5: 22, 23) can mean judgment (depending on the circumstances in the dream)
10	=	To be tested, wilderness, a trial; temptation (Rev. 2:10); law, gov't, can also mean acceptable or unacceptable in quality

---

[3] "The Ultimate Guide To Understanding the Dreams You Dream" by Ira Milligan page 239

11	=	Disorder, transition, end, finish; last stop (Gen. 32:22; Dan. 7:24)

12 = United to govern; government (Luke 9:12; Luke 22:30)

13 = Rebellion, revolutionary change; rejection (Gen.14: 4)

14 = Double, reproduce, recreate, disciple, a servant bond slave (2 Kings 8:65); double anointing.

15 = Grace, mercy, free, liberty, salvation; sin covered; honor (2 Kings 20: 6; Hosea 3:2)

16 = Free spirited; without law; without boundaries, salvation (Acts 27:34-38); renewing relations with God.

17 = Unfinished, immature, babe in Christ (negative) (Gen. 37:2); Perfection of spiritual order walking with God (positive)

18 = Putting on the Spirit of Christ, to overcome (Luke 13:11,16) (positive); can mean judgment; in captivity.

19 = Barren, ashamed, repentant, selflessness, without self-righteousness.

20 = Holy, tried and approved (Rev. 4:4)

100 = Fullness, of full measure, full reward (Gen. 26:12)

1000 = Maturity: full stature, mature service (positive) (Eph. 4:13); can mean mature judgment (negative).

ANOTHER EXERCISE ON INTERPRETING DREAMS AND NUMBERS

Interpret the following dream: A dream revealed in May 2008:

> *"I was at an altar observing 5 white lit candlesticks on a lamp stand and a tall stack of Showbread containers made of gold on a stick (Interpret and analyze the dream). (Check your diagram answer on page 54).*

What is the dreamer doing?: *(Observing or Participating)*	
Main Focus:	
Sub Focus:	

Detail(s): *(Includes color, muted, Black and White, darkness, light, etc.)*	
Title:	
Category:	
Interpret or research the symbolic words:	
What does the dream mean? *(Consult the Holy Spirit)*	

CHAPTER 7

WHEN GOD BECOMES SILENT

For about every three months, I would not receive dreams nor visions. If I did receive even a mini-dream by the Spirit, it was every now and then. Usually, I would receive dreams more than once in a month. I sometimes ask God, why He doesn't speak to me often any more in dreams and visions like He use to. I started to think that perhaps I was not speaking in tongues enough nor spending ample private time with Him or maybe I was not getting the proper sleep. I notice I have become a light sleeper now that I am getting up in age.

I've been noticing that the more I speak in tongues, the more God started to speak to me in a still small voice in my waking state, as if someone was speaking in my spiritual ear. He now gives me more mini-visions and I rarely have dreams with more than one scene in them. I will never forget that mini-visions given by God are just as significant as lengthy dreams. They say a whole lot in a message. Remember, God speaking to you by a still small voice and in visions in your waking state are the highest form of communication other than dreams. Dreams are the simplest level of how God speaks to man when he is still and not busily active.

Perhaps God is teaching me how to hear Him not only in my dreams, but in my waking state which had not been happening enough in the past. Since I am basically a light sleeper, when I am half asleep or in a twilight state of consciousness that is when the Holy Spirit reveals mini-visions to me. This happens after I pray in tongues for about 15 or more minutes.

So when you think God has been silent because He's not speaking to you in dreams and visions, or you have come to that season in your life when God seems to be silent, He could be inspiring you to seek Him more or to chase after Him more in your quest for Him. Do the following:

1. Seek the Lord and ask Him why He has become silent. This lets God know you are really seeking to fellowship with Him more.

2. Pray in the Spirit often either in your native language or in your devotional spiritual language called speaking in tongues as you sit still in His Presence. You will be stirring up His presence within your spirit and becoming more sensitive to Him. God says in His Word to be still and know He is God within you. You can pray in the Spirit even when you drive your car, or do daily chores. He can speak and respond to you.

3. When God seems silent, it is His way of wetting your appetite to relate to Him on another spiritual level of hearing Him, such as hearing Him by a still small voice often while you are awake. If you hear Him in this way, you will have the faith to act on what He tells you without a doubt. You can expect Him to answer you and confirm what He said to you not only within yourself, but through a vision, dream, another spiritual person, minister or a prophet. Stand firm on what you heard the Lord say to you. Don't back down. This is your faith in activation.

4. When God seems silent, it leads you to keep your focus on Him with anticipation and expectation, even when circumstances seem to be the opposite of what you see or expect. Read the story of the vision Habakkuk had concerning the length of time he had to wait for an answer from God to save him and the Jews from his enemies in Hab. 1:2-4, and what he did to expect an answer from Him about a second question he had concerning the attack of the Babylonian empire in Hab. 2:1,2. God did not answer Habakkuk right away, so he sought and waited on God

to receive a response from God no matter how long it took. Notice too, God's silence to answer Habakkuk in Hab. 1:1,2, led him to seek God for deliverance from his enemies by asking persistent questions.

5. When God seems silent, it could be because you are looking too much towards prophets to give you direction from God, when God wants you to learn to hear Him for yourself. Prophecy spoken over you should most of the time, confirm what God has already told you. If God has not confirmed this prophecy spoken over you, then wait on it. Do not act on it. If it does not come to pass in about 5-10 years, then ignore it, however, seek the Lord in prayer about the prophecy. James 1:5, 6a says (NAS ed.), "But if any of you lacks wisdom, let him ask of God, who gives to all men generously and without reproach, and it will be given to him. But let him ask in faith without any doubting…"

6. When you have come into a dry season and when God seems silent, know that He is still with you. He has not forsaken you. When you continue to pursue Him through prayer and reading His Word, He will satisfy your heart by drawing you closer to Him, so walk by faith and not by sight. Reflect on dreams He did reveal to you last and expect more from Him.

In the times when God wants to reveal something to you, He will tell you in a dream, vision or in a waking state by a still small voice. Again, since I have been speaking more in tongues, I have been receiving more mini-visions, at least twice a month and hearing a still small voice sometimes concerning a political leader or ISIS (who God impressed upon my spirit on Dec. 24, 2016 at about 1 p.m. that its days are numbered).

Answer the following questions on another sheet of paper:

1. How often do I dream or have visions or hear a still small voice? (If none, ask God in prayer to reveal and speak to you more in dreams and visions or even speak to you by a still small voice).

2. If God has revealed dreams in the past or has spoken to you in your waking state, about when did God become silent to you? How long was the silence?

3. What have you learned to apply when you come to a dry season when God has become silent? Write down what you would do.

Once your dreams, visions or even the ability to hear God's still small voice return, keep a journal of what God says to you once you have searched and consulted the Holy Spirit for the meaning of what was said. Do not be concerned if God is silent every now and then. Remember, He is taking you and I to another spiritual level of communication, especially when we are in our waking state which again is the highest form of God communicating with us.

CHAPTER 8

10 EXERCISES ON INTERPRETING MORE DREAMS AND REVELATIONS OF THINGS

1. Ask God to give more revelation knowledge as to how He would relay to you a message of the following objects and expand their meaning (Journal God's response in your notebook or another sheet of paper with date).

   A) The spring water flowing
   B) A light bulb shining in a room
   C) A tall tree near the pond of water
   D) An eagle soaring
   E) An emerald stone

2. Interpret the following dreams below determining where the dreamer is, the focus, the sub focus, details, the colors, whether it's dark or light dream, the theme, the category, interpret the symbols (use your dream dictionaries), and determine the meaning of the dreams by the Holy Spirit's impressions, thoughts that come to you or a still small voice. Write them on another sheet of paper: (The dreamer is the author of this book)

   A) A dream revealed in Mar. 2006: On Monday morning, March 27, 2006, the dreamer was having devotional time in the Presence of God. She had a vision that she was observing a silver ring with 3 oval shaped diamond stones situated like a clover leaf on the ring. All 3 stones glittered on the ring.

B) 2 scenes in one Dream revealed in Feb. 2007: The dreamer dreamed in scene 1 that she was wading in a river of water with long rubber boots on. The river turned to the color of gold or amber, like as the glory of God, warming the river. Then the dream changed into another scene.

Scene 2 The dreamer and other Christians dressed in white attire were fellowshipping and sitting in the house of God full of light. A male Christian opened the door of the Church. Outside was very dark at night with headlights of cars beaming. A mist like dew fell from the sky. People were running to and fro in a panic in the atmosphere that was full of the mist. One man was running with a garbage can that consumed in his hand by the mist. The dream ended.

C) An Open Vision revealed on Feb. 22, 2010: The dreamer had an open vision or outward vision of carrying a basket or a container of a mixture of raspberries, and blueberries to a section in Pathmark supermarket. The vision changed to the dreamer getting up from sitting on a group of green grapes. (This vision has come to pass and still coming to pass).

D) A dream revealed on Fri. April 16, 2010: Dreamer had a morning dream of many, many Christians dressed in white attire on a college campus. Ladies were dressed in 19 cent. white gowns. The first three ladies wore large wide brimmed white hats decorated with large lily flowers with the sign of a cross inside each flower. The other ladies on the campus wore the same apparel. The men wore white suits with white shoes. They were all standing in an oval shaped line on the campus facing the dreamer as the dreamer observed them looking at her and walking towards her. They were all dressed in white preparing to meet their Bridegroom at the same time looking at the dreamer.

E) A dream revealed on Wed. Nov. 23, 2016: Based on homework assignment by the dreamer's instructor on the topic of a "stream of water flowing." God revealed to the dreamer and fulfilled her assignment in a dream: The dreamer observed a stream of clear water flowing and rippling on the dirt full of smooth rocks. The stream was surrounded by a dark forest in the background. It was not a sunny day. The dream ended.

THE MEANING OF THE DREAMS GIVEN

The meaning of the dreams given on pages 45-50 may agree with your interpretation of the symbols and meaning of the dreams. The interpretation of the symbols and the meaning of each dream are as follows:

For Dream "A":

What is the dreamer doing?: Observing

Main Focus: The Silver Ring

Sub focus: 3 oval shape diamond stones

Detail(s): the stones glittered. It was in color

Title: The Silver Ring

Category: A Covenant and Promising Dream

Interpretation of Symbols:

The Silver Ring = A redemptive covenant
3 stones = Trinity, three persons (Father, Son & Holy Spirit) Oval shape
diamond = completely precious
Stones glittered = The reflection of the Holy Spirit

The meaning of the dream: The dreamer has a redemptive covenant with the Father, Son and the Holy Spirit and therefore, she is precious, solid or secure in the Godhead and radiant with the Holy Spirit living within her.

For Dream "B":
(Had 2 scenes)

Scene 1: ***What is the dreamer doing?:*** Participating

Main Focus: The Dreamer

Sub focus: wading in the river

Detail(s): long boots; gold; warm; It was in color

Title: A Dreamer's Mission;

Category: Calling Dream scene 1.

Interpretation of symbols: wading in the river (walking in the Holy Spirit); long boots = taking the Gospel to the nations, protection, spiritual warfare; gold = glory, deeds done in the Holy Spirit; warm = power of God.

Meaning of the Dream: As the dreamer continues to walk or live by and in the Holy Spirit, God will empower her to take and teach His Word wherever He sends her, protecting her from those who come against her in word and deed.

Scene 2: ***What is the dreamer doing?***: Participating

Main Focus: The Dreamer;

Sub focus: Other Christians, House of God of light; Fellowshipping with one another; a Male Christian; open front door of the Church; Dream was in color.

Detail(s): Mist like dew; dark night; headlights of cars (black and white); people running in panic; man with garbage pail consumed.

Title: A Divine Shaking Coming; Theme: Preparation For the Church to be used

Category: A Calling Dream For the Church body; a Revival dream also.

Interpreting the symbols:

Dreamer and Christians clothed in white = God's remnant Church body;
House of God of light = The Kingdom of God; Church body;
A Male Christian = Jesus Christ, open front door of the Church
= Church body facing an opportunity to do a future task for Christ;
Fellowshipping with one another = together in unity.
Mist or dew = a spiritual invasion of the Holy Spirit; a spiritual transition; a spiritual shaking.
People running in panic = humanity in confusion, fear.
Man with garbage pail consumed = the sin of such a man is judged and/ or delivered from sin.
Headlights of cars in black and white colors = trouble; in a time of crisis.
Dark night = atmosphere in chaotic state.

Meaning of Scene 2 of the dream: The Body of Christ, the remnant Church is to come together in unity to prepare by the direction of Jesus Christ, to be a part of a move of the Holy Spirit, that will shake the nations and all of humanity. This will cause nations to either to receive Christ as their personal savior, by our witness of salvation or receive the judgment of God which will cause fear and confusion amongst unbelievers who don't know the spiritual things of God nor understand the move of the Holy Spirit.

You can see that the meaning of the dream in the first scene is related to the meaning of the dream in the second scene in that they are both Calling scenes in one dream. The dreamer in scene 1 and the body of Christ in scene 2 are called to prepare to be used of the Holy Spirit to share the message of salvation in the time of crisis in our nation. The body of Christ will suffer opposition, however, the power of God of the Holy Spirit within the Christians and the angels, as well as the use of the Word of God in our mouths, will protect the Christians. The remnant body of Christ is to work together in unity to promote the call of Jesus Christ doing the Great Commission, that is, sharing the Gospel and healing the sick.

Dream "C":

What is the dreamer doing? Participating

Main Focus: The Dreamer;

Sub focus: The basket, green grapes, raspberries, blueberries, Pathmark supermarket

Detail(s): getting up from sitting; the vision was in color,

The Title: Being Fruitful;

Category: Encouraging vision; A calling vision

Interpreting the Symbols: basket = contains blessings within, fruitfulness = represents the dreamer; raspberries, blueberries, and green grapes = fruit of the Word of God; Pathmark supermarket section = a small church of a group of people, a small ministry; getting up from sitting on the green grapes = doing kingdom business; teaching the fruitful Word to others, given authority (sitting); in other words, getting up and going to share and teach the Word of God in His authority.

Meaning of the vision (in 2 parts) Part 1. The dreamer contains within her (the basket) the blessing and fruitfulness of God's Word. She is to take the Word and teach it to first, to small groups of people in Churches (section in Pathmark supermarket); Part 2 – the dreamer will then be inspired by God to take her teaching to the nations, or wherever God directs her to get up and go to. She will take her teaching of the Word in the authority of Christ. This two part vision has already started to come to pass. Presently, I am teaching a small group of people at my Bible Discussion group and teaching at a small beginning Bible College, called Christ For The World International Bible College in St. Albans, N.Y. I expect God to expand me and spread my spiritual wings to take my teaching ability to other church communities and nations.

Dream "D":

What is the dreamer doing? Observing while sitting on a large rock.

Main Focus: Men and women dressed in white;

Sub focus: ladies wearing 19th century gowns and white lily big brimmed hats; men wore white suits and shoes.

Detail(s): College campus; standing in an oval shaped line; staring at the dreamer. The dream was in color; it was a sunny day;

Title: Getting Ready For The King.

Categories: Encouraging; a Calling dream; a dream of preparation.

Interpreting the symbols: Observer sitting on a large rock = resting in Jesus Christ who is the Rock; men and women dressed in white = the Church body in Christ. Ladies wearing 19 century gowns and large brimmed hats = to signify holiness and righteousness in the sight of God; lily hats signify = the covering of the blood and love of Jesus Christ. Men wearing white suits and shoes = signifies walking in the authority of God or as a leader of God; college campus= an institute for learning; men and women standing in an oval shaped line = Church body ready to be taught in unity; looking at the dreamer = waiting to be taught by the dreamer.

Meaning of the dream: Those who are saved, sanctified and filled with the Spirit of God, like the days of the first awakening of the Christians in the late 19 and early 20th century people, there was a great move of the Holy Spirit. In this dream, the body of Christ who are filled with the Holy Spirit and His righteousness are waiting in line in unity on a College campus ready to be taught concerning the coming of our Lord Jesus and being prepared to be raptured. They look to the dreamer who is in the teaching strength and guidance of Jesus Christ to prepare them for the coming King through the teaching and study of the Signs of the Times. This dream has come to pass. The dreamer presently is teaching on the study of the Book of Revelation at the small college stated above and on youtube.com. She has written a book called,

"Eschatology: The Signs of the Times of Jesus Christ's Soon Return". His Coming Is Closer Than You Think". To purchase the book, consult Amazon.com, Barnes and Nobles.com, or you can contact any Christian bookstore to order the book for you, or you can contact my website: www.thegreatcommissionmultiservice.org to order the reference book.

Dream "E":

What is the dreamer doing? Observing *Main Focus:* A flowing stream of clear water: *Sub focus:* smooth stones or rocks.

Detail(s): dark forest; inclement day; dark with some light; dirt, muted dream

Title: The Flowing Stream of Water;

Category: A Prophetic dream; encouraging dream

Interpreting the symbols: Clear stream of water flowing = the move of the Holy Spirit; smooth stones or rocks = represents Christians; surrounded by a dark forest = confusion of humanity; trouble in a nation or community; inclement day=a day of uncertainty amongst the people; dark with some light= the presence of God invading the confusion amongst humanity; dirt = the land, earth

What does the dream mean? There will be an outpouring and move of the Holy Spirit that will flow through the Christians witnessing the gospel or the Word of God throughout the land or nation, all over the earth where there is confusion or in a time of crisis in the land. There will be a revival in the land. It is coming soon.

If your interpretation of the given dreams above is somewhat agreeable with the interpretation of the dreams by the author, you are on your way to being an effective dream interpreter. The dreams from A to E were actual visions or dreams that the author had of which three came to pass, dream "A", dream "C" and dream "D". Dream "B" and dream "E" are prophetic and will soon come to pass in the U.S.A. In fact, dream "B" and dream "E" have already received the outpouring and move of the Holy Spirit and the spread of the gospel in communistic nations such as the Middle East and Asian nations.

More answer diagrams to dreams:

Dream 1 on page 25 - Diagram dream answers:

What is the dreamer doing? Observing **Main Focus:** The Padlock

Sub Focus: The Chain, The Ruby

Details: gold, red, center

Symbolic meanings: The Padlock = Security, Sealed, Chain = joined together in the Spirit, Ruby = precious, Jesus Christ, Red = blood covenant, Gold = Majestic, glory, Center = importance, to depend on, deeply involved, divine order.

Title: The Precious Padlock

Category: Encouraging and calling dream

Interpretation: The dreamer or Christian in general, is precious to God. He or she is joined together with Jesus Christ in the Spirit by His blood covenant and by His Holy Spirit who is the glory of Christ. For He is the center of the Christian life.

Dream 2 on page 25 - Diagram dream answers:

What is the dreamer doing? Observing

Main Focus: Animated figure of Jesus Christ's Head

Sub Focus: Pieces of hail, fiery stars, Jesus blew wind

Details: blue, sky

Symbolic meanings: Animated Head of Jesus Christ = to relate the figure to the nature and character of the person, hails = Christians asleep in spirit, or in a complacent state; Jesus blew wind on the hails = represents the Holy Spirit reawakening, Stars of fire = The dreamer or Christian is reawakened or revived by the Holy Spirit of glory.

Title: The Last Awakening

Category: A prophetic Dream

Interpretation: The person of Jesus Christ will initiate the Holy Spirit to reawaken the Christians who tend to be complacent about the things of God. Those Christians who are sensitive to the move of the Holy Spirit will be empowered by the fire of the Holy Spirit to be effective witnesses for Christ and do exploits and be spiritually directed by God of heaven.

Dream 1 on page 33 - Diagram dream answers:

What is the dreamer doing? Observing

Main Focus: The map of the U.S.A.

Sub Focus: U.S.A. displaced and paced on the map at Saudi Arabia in the Middle East.

Details: The color green of U.S.A.

Symbolic meanings: Map of U.S.A. = God's plan for America, the target is America U.S.A. displaced = a judgment shift U.S.A. placed on the map of Saudi Arabia or Middle East = America has been influenced and invaded by the Muslim agenda and doctrine of Islam, Green (with white) = is the color of Saudi Arabia's banners. **Title:** The Invasion of Islam in America

Category: A judgment dream, a warning dream, a correction dream.

Interpretation: Since America has strayed away from the statutes of God, God has allowed the invasion of Muslim agenda threaten our country. The doctrine of Islam has infiltrated into the public high schools and colleges, into the liberal churches of today mixing Islam with Christianity called Chrislam, and the Sharia Law working alongside with the Constitution of our nation in our judicial system. America has experienced numerous attacks by jahad extremists and have spread their political and religious agenda through immigration.

Dream 2 on page 34 - Dream diagram answers:

What is the dreamer doing? Observing

Main Focus: U.S.A.

Sub Focus: Small Cars moving around shape of America; glory of God

Details: All black U.S.A., on global map

Symbolic meanings: U.S.A. on a global map = Attention on America, small cars going around the shape of America = Christians are called to minister to Americans in need in time of trouble around the world, the glory upon the small cars = the cars will reflect the glory and the empowerment of God, the black U.S.A. = Americans who are perplexed, confused and troubled during a time of crisis.

Title: Doing The Great Commission of the Body of Christ

Category: A calling dream, a prophetic dream

Interpretation: The Body of Christ around the world is to share the gospel, heal the sick and operate in the gifts of the Spirit and minister to Americans who are confused, sick and perplexed during a time of crisis that will increase in our nation.

Dream on page 37 concerning a number "5" - Dream diagram answers:

What is the dreamer doing? Participating and observing

Main Focus: The Dreamer

Sub Focus: The lampstand of 5 candles, the showbread containers

Details: White candles, gold containers, the altar and the stick

Symbolic meanings: The Dreamer = A representative of Jesus Christ, 5 white candlesticks on a lampstand = 5 churches of righteousness, dreamer at the altar = dreamer sacrifices her service, showbread in gold containers on a stick= the written word of God lifted up by the Holy Spirit

Title: Serving 5 Churches of Good Standing **Category:** A calling dream

Interpretation: The dreamer sacrifices herself to be a blessing and minister serving 5 churches of good standing teaching the Word of God that is inspired by the Holy Spirit so that Jesus Christ may be lifted up for people to see and hear.

CONCLUSION

It is hoped that this handbook of understanding your dreams has been helpful to you, and that you will study and practice what you have learned in order to understand and interpret your dreams and visions with confidence. You will not only have the ability to interpret your own dreams, but interpret the dreams of other people as well. God loves to communicate and share secrets with you, because He loves you. He loves you, because He created you in your mother's womb. If you have accepted His Son, Jesus Christ, as your personal Savior, you will have great access to the wisdom and knowledge of God through dreams and visions which are the normal ways God can communicate with you while you sleep.

However, the highest way God communicates is when you are awake by a still small voice, by an impression or inward knowing, or you may have an inner peace about something as a sign that God has unctioned you to say or do something. If you do not have peace about something, it is a sign by God, within you not to say or do something. God also communicates when thoughts or ideas come to you.

Continue to practice the exercises in this handbook to stimulate your ability to interpret dreams and visions. Practice the presence of God by praying in the Spirit, engaging in praise and worship, and reading scriptures from a devotional book or Bible, or hearing a sermon on CD's or DVD's, etc. This is so that God can share with you his revelatory knowledge when you are alone with Him. When this happens, do not forget to write down what God says to you in your dreams, visions and in your waking state. Continue to use the format suggested in this handbook to interpret your dreams and visions. When journaling, ask God to reveal to you images. Ask Him what they mean and how do they apply to you.

The Holy Spirit is the revelator within a Christian. He is real within you. He is a person within you. He hears and lives within you. So talk to Him like a buddy. He will reveal what you ask of Him. He loves to talk to you and reveal things to you. So trust Him to answer you. He may reveal things to you in a dream, either in an open or closed vision, in a trance, in your waking state as a still small voice, or as an impression or ideas that come to your spirit. Unbelievers can have this same communication experience with God if they choose to accept Jesus Christ as their personal Savior. Just call on the name of Jesus to come into your heart and His Spirit will connect you to the true God of the Universe. You will automatically be God's son or daughter. Get in a good church that teaches about Jesus Christ and about the Holy Spirit. In Christ, old things and the way you used to think are passed away; behold all things have become new. You become a new creature in Christ. 2Corinthians 5:17. You will make mistakes while growing in the things of God, however, repent of them quickly and go on learning what is in the Bible to help you live the Christian way of life. Go to Bible studies at a church of your choice or conferences to be with other Christians.

God still loves the unbeliever and backslider and calls them to come to Jesus Christ, His Son. Whoever has the Son in his or her heart, has Eternal Life. It is by Jesus Christ's Spirit, the Holy Spirit that you have the ability to communicate with the true God and God with you. For God is a Spirit and He is one with you through Jesus Christ. He communicates to you in your redeemed spirit, of which your soul and mind identifies. Therefore, by faith you are able to obey what the Spirit of God says to you as you speak, write, act out what God unctions you to say or do through a dream, vision, by a still small voice within or by impressions in a waking state.

BOOK RESOURCES

1. The New King James Bible
2. Understanding Dreams & Visions Workbook, by Pro. John Paul Jackson, copyright 1979, 1980, 1982, by Thomas Nelson Inc. - ISBN 1-58483-025-5
3. The Ultimate Guide To Understanding The Dreams You Dream, by Ira Milligan copyright 2012, Destiny Image Publisher - ISBN 13 Ebook: 978-0-7684-8859-3
4. Dream Language (The Prophetic Power of Dreams, Revelation, and the spirit of wisdom), by James W & Michal Ann Goll, copyright 2006
   Destiny Image Publishers, Inc. - ISBN 13-978-0-7684-2354- 9

BIBLICALLY BASED DREAM DICTIONARIES

1. The Ultimate Guide To Understanding The Dreams You Dream, by Ira Milligan, copyright 2012
2. Dictionary of Dream Symbols (The illustrated Bible Based), by Dr. Joe Ibojie, copyright 2005, Destiny Image, Europe srl - ISBN 13-978-88- 89127-14-8
3. The Divinity Code (To Understanding Your Dreams and Visions), by Adam F. Thompson & Adrian Beale, Copyright

CD'S AND DVD'S RESOURCES

Dreams & Mysteries Volumes 1 & 2 of 3 DVD's by Streams Ministries International, CEO and founder, Pro. & Teacher, John Paul Jackson; www.dreamsandmysteries.com or www.streamsministries.com

1. The Biblical Model of Dream Interpretation
   (Avoiding the Pitfalls of Soulish Methodology) By Pro. & Teacher, John Paul Jackson, founder of Streams Ministries Int'l

A SHORT RESUME OF THE AUTHOR: Rev. Sandra Yvonne Washington is an ordained Minister of the Gospel by the International Congress Of Churches and Ministers, Dr. Michael Chitwood, CEO and by the Christ For The World International Ministries, Apostle Bobby Hogan, overseer and Bishop David Butler, N.Y. Site overseer of the Christ For The World International Bible College under whom she serves as a professor, teaching the Book of Revelation, Holy Spirit and His Spiritual Gifts with activation, Eschatology and Understanding Your Dreams and Visions And Interpreting Them. Rev. Washington is the Executive Director of her own ministry, The Great Commission Multi-Service Community Center, Inc. which is an outreach ministry to help build the body of Christ teaching it to do the Great Commission stated in Mark 16:15-18; and help prepare the body of Christ for the coming of Jesus Christ at the Rapture event through the teaching of Eschatology.

Rev. Washington has been divinely inspired not only as a singer, author, and teacher of the Gospel, but as a developing prophetic seer in the area of dreams and visions with the developing ability to interpret them. It is her desire to write this handbook on understanding your dreams and visions for those who wish to understand their dreams and visions and to be able to interpret them.

This handbook is also written for those who have the potential of becoming a prophetic seer and who have been called by God to develop the seer gift, especially, when God communicates with the individual who has received Christ's Spirit called the Holy Spirit in their hearts in which the Holy Spirit reveals things to your spirit through dreams and visions while asleep or awake very often. This experience only comes about when one establishes intimacy with Jesus Christ by way of his or her communion with the Holy Spirit.

Further Prophetic Ministry Development:

1. Christian International School of Theology, received M.S. Deg. in Ministry (Prophetic Maj.) May, 2009; Pro. Bill Hamon, founder in Santa Rosa Beach, FL.
2. Bethel Supernatural School of Ministry, received a 2 year Diploma, June, 2016, Pro. Paulette Polo, instructor in Cranford, N.J. 07016
3. Naioth Prophetical Arts Institute, presently attending until June 2017; Pro. Teresa Gripper, founder and instructor in Brooklyn, N.Y. 11213

Further Study of Dreams and Visions with Interpretation Development:

1. Streams Ministries International; under the tutelage of Pro. John Paul Jackson and his assistant teachers within a period of 3 years from about 2002 to 2005; Pro. John Paul Jackson (deceased in 2015) founder and instructor in New Hampshire; headquarters moved to Lewisville, TX. 75067.
2. Kingdom Training Institute. Took classes on Interpreting dreams for about one year; Min. Russ Painter, founder; Rev. Gary Fishman, instructor in Cranford, N.J. 07016
3. Naioth prophetical Arts Institute. Completed a semester course on Dreams and Visions with interpretation from Oct. 2016 to Dec. 2016. Pro. Teresa Gripper, CEO & instructor in Brooklyn, N.Y. 11213.

www.ingramcontent.com/pod-product-compliance
Lightning Source LLC
Chambersburg PA
CBHW051238120626
46547CB00014B/1702